Harbingers

Books and Chapbooks by Elisavietta Ritchie

TIMBOT revised edition, Shelden Studios, novella-in-verse (2017)
REFLECTIONS: PAINTINGS & POEMS, FROM A POET'S GALLERY
   Poets' Choice Publishers (2017)
BABUSHKA'S BEADS: A GEOGRAPHY OF GENES
   Poets' Choice Publishers (2016)
GUY WIRES Poets' Choice Publishers (2015)
IN HASTE I WRITE YOU THIS NOTE: STORIES & HALF-STORIES
   Washington Writers' Publishing House (e-book 2015)
TIGER UPSTAIRS ON CONNECTICUT AVENUE
   (Cherry Grove Collections, WordTech Communications (2013)
FEATHERS, OR, LOVE ON THE WING
   Shelden Studios, collaboration with artists Megan Richard, Suzanne Shelden (2013)
FROM THE ARTIST'S DEATHBED Winterhawk Press (chapbook 2012)
CORMORANT BEYOND THE COMPOST Cherry Grove Collections (2011)
REAL TOADS Black Buzzard Press (chapbook, 2008)
AWAITING PERMISSION TO LAND Cherry Grove Collections (2006)
THE SPIRIT OF THE WALRUS Bright Hill Press (chapbook 2005)
IN HASTE I WRITE YOU THIS NOTE: STORIES & HALF-STORIES,
   Washington Writers' Publishing House (2000)
THE ARC OF THE STORM Signal Books (1998)
ELEGY FOR THE OTHER WOMAN: NEW & SELECTED POEMS
   Signal Books (1996)
WILD GARLIC: THE JOURNAL OF MARIA X.
   Harper Collins (novella in verse, chapbook 1995)
A WOUND-UP CAT AND OTHER BEDTIME STORIES
   Palmerston Press (chapbook, 1993)
FLYING TIME: STORIES & HALF-STORIES Signal Books (1986, 1988)
THE PROBLEM WITH EDEN Armstrong State College Press, (chapbook 1985)
RAKING THE SNOW Washington Writers' Publishing House (1982)
A SHEATH OF DREAMS & OTHER GAMES Proteus Press (chapbook 1976)
TIGHTENING THE CIRCLE OVER EEL COUNTRY Acropolis Books (1974)

Poetry Anthologies Edited:

THE DOLPHIN'S ARC: Poems on Endangered Creatures of the Sea
   SCOP (1986)
FINDING THE NAME Wineberry Press (1983)

Harbingers

Elisavietta Ritchie

Poets' Choice Publishing

Copyright © 2017 Poets' Choice Publishing
All rights reserved
Printed in the United States of America

Author's photo: Alexander Farnsworth

Consultant work:
www.WilliamMeredithFoundation.org

Bulk discounts available through www.Poets-choice.com

Library of Congress Cataloging-in-Publication Data pending
ISBN 978-0-9972629-6-4

Poets' Choice Publishing
337 Kitemaug Road
Uncasville, CT 06382
Poets-Choice.com

In flight toward? away?
I'm caught in clouds, floating
between heaven and hell.

ACKNOWLEDGMENTS

We wish to thank the editors of these journals and anthologies who first published these poems, most in earlier versions:

"A DOG in my SPAM?": *And the Tail Wagged On*, anthology, Harry Yang, editor, Lost Tower Publications, September 2015;

"After Departures": *Home Planet News*, circa 1980;

"An Arial Ballet: Salome": *International Dance Journal*, Supplement II. circa 1980;

"Arboreal Identifications:"The Broadkill Review, 2017, editor Jaime Brown;

"A Real Big Mother Terrapin": *The Bay Weekly*, August 12, 2016, editor Sandra Martin;

"Between Two Thunderstorms": *Prosopisia*, anthology editors Anuraag Sharma & Moizur Rehman Khan, Summer, 2015;

"Cake-Eaters:" *Prosopisia*, Summer, 2015;

"Cat Tracks:" *Visions*, no. 9, editor Brad Strahan, 1982; "Credo": *Home Planet News* (?) circa 1977;

"Crossing the Field": *Northeast Journal*, vol. 2, no. 2, 1981;

"Determinations": *Home Planet News*, April 1980;

"Discussing Olympus at the Nursing Home": *Operative*, fall/winter, circa 1980; *Texture*, Summer 2017, editor Cliff Lynn;

"Egg-Collecting": *Ann Arbor Review*, 1975, editor Fred Wolven; "Endeavoring": *Ann Arbor Review*, 2017;

"Exoskeletons": *Earth's Daughters*, 2017; *Prosopisia*, 2017;

"Expiration Dates:" *Ann Arbor Review*, 2017;

"Galaxy: Another Archetypal Love Poem": *Prosopisia*, Summer, 2015;

"Gardeners in Flight": *Ann Arbor Review*, 2016;

"Infolding": *Ann Arbor Review*, 1975;

"Like Ghandi, I'll Observe a Day of Silence": *Ann Arbor Review*, 2016;

"Our Housemate from India Asks": *Earth's Daughters*, 2017; *Prosopisia*, 2017;

"Pushing Through the Night": *Ann Arbor Review*, 2017;

"Sandcave Summer": *Ann Arbor Review*, 2016;

"Strange Nightly Visitors": *Ann Arbor Review*, 2017;

"Tiger Lilies": The Broadkill Review, 2017; *The Poetry of Flowers*, Harry Yang, anthology editor, Lost Tower Publications, 2016;

"Tradecraft: Finding a Safehouse for a Flower": *Ann Arbor Review*, 2016;

"Trying to Make Connections": *Ann Arbor Review*, 2016;

"We Wake Beside an Invisible River": *The Broadkill Review*, 2017; *Prosopisia*, 2017;

"When Foxes Came Calling": *The Bay Weekly*, 12-21 September 2016;

"Winged Visitations": *Prosopisia*, Summer, 2015;

"You Missed Two Young Bald Eagles...": Ann Arbor Review, 2017; *Prosopisia*, 2017.

To
Elspeth Cameron Ritchie
Lyell Kirk Ritchie
Alexander George Ritchie

CONTENTS

I. Waiting for Wisdom

Losers, Weepers   3
Waiting on the Dock for Wisdom   4
Like Ghandi, I'll Observe a Day of Silence   6
Identity Check   7
Endeavoring   8
Sandcave Summer   9
Coffin Sales   11
Expiration Dates   12
Anton, My Sweet   13
Photo of the Artist as a Double Exposure   15
My Twenty-Ninth Draft   16

II. Country Matters

Trying to Make Connections   19
We Wake Beside an Invisible River   21
Winged Visitations   23
Exoskeletons   24
Strange Nightly Visitors   26
Trying to Nab Him   27
When Foxes Came Calling   29
Between Two Thunderstorms: Floricultural Traditions   30
A Real Big Mother Terrapin   32
Natural Questions   33
Fifty Beans   34
Cake-Eaters   35
Arboreal   36
Farmer's Almanac Forecasts   37
Gardeners in Flight   38
You Missed Two Young Eagles   39

III. Foreign Affairs

Like a Flame from the Hearth, Love— 43
Infolding 44
Egg-Collecting 45
Do You See Colors Coming? 47
Setting History Straight 49
Tradecraft: Finding a Safe House 51
Our Housemate from India Asks 52
"Psychiatrists Inspect Your Purse" 53
Old Housemates 54
Real Estate Stationary 55
A Dog in My SPAM? 56
"Legs and Toes in Ancestor of Living Snakes" 57
Those Lights 58
Skullduggery 59
Today the Roofer— 61
Dissolution Rates: The Mouse in the Toilet 63
Galaxy: Another Archetypal Love Poem 65
Pushing Through the Night 66
Relentless Mind 67
After Departures 68
Cat Tracks 69
Crossing the Field 71
An Aerial Ballet 72
Determinations 73
Discussing Olympus at the Nursing Home 74
August at the County Landfill 76
Credo 77

AUTHOR'S NOTE 79

I
Waiting for Wisdom

Losers, Weepers

What was that poem lost at midnight
by my not writing it down

Splinters from the dock
pierced the bloody moon

Tomato juice or blood
spurted across the sky

On the dock at dawn
twelve flat beige seeds

but no words

Waiting on the Dock for Wisdom

I swat mosquitoes,
try to banish
that meddler, Thought.

A swallow swoops
to her mud nest
beneath these planks.

The heron stalks
shallows for minnows,
probes flats for clams.

Claws wide,
the osprey plummets,
spears a flounder,
then perches atop
the dead sycamore,
tears apart the flesh.

None of these winged
messengers reveal
whatever omens in entrails,
nor bring insight
nor announce miracles.

Sudden thunder –
Lightning strikes a pine –
Torrents of rain

Soaked, cold,
I flee indoors.

Perhaps I'll find
enlightenment in sparks
from a fire in the hearth,
tea laced with rum.

Like Gandhi, I'll Observe a Day of Silence

But suddenly cicadas all at once turn on—
Discarded exoskeletons crunch like potato chips—

Swans hiss, herons croak, gulls shriek, wrens shrill—
Frogs in the marsh discuss romance—

Fear of silence wraps me like a shroud…
Beethoven's Ninth! Full voice I sing along.

Identity Check

Not yet sure who I am.

Though some consider me
eccentric, at least on the edge
of the vortex of events,
I missed becoming a hippie.

Too late now to become
a third-generation punk
with pink hair and pierced skin:
six earrings per lobe, navel and tongue,
miniskirt over bare knees.

Nor am I an academic
with horn-rimmed specs
scholarly strings of letters
I cannot decipher
after my name.

Better be a 21st Century Mata Hari
in a souk, a veiled vendor of figs
with cyber- ciphering skills
and access to secret files on the Internet.

Most who suffer identity complexes
have insurance to cover expensive pills.

Others are merely writers and seers.

Endeavoring

A brown moth beats against the screen.
The same or similar each night.

I too want to get in, understand
what's happening inside. I can't

enlighten anyone, but like the moth
slap wings against the pane.

Condemned to stay outside,
I'll wave furry antennae,

beat my shreds of wings as if,
once inside, I could figure it all out…

Sandcave Summer

That summer my first love and I
lived in a cave we dug in an old
pit near Three Rivers, Wisconsin.

Five years old, under a roof of reeds
spread across our stick frame,
we lay close the way parents do,

My love's diabetic brother, seven,
who every day got shots from the nurse,
tunneled his own cave next door.

Beyond our forbidden quarry,
pastures stretched past the creek,
field corn rose higher and higher.

We lost ourselves in forests of stalks,
then reset our compass, plotted a course
back to our cave, ate our apples and bread.

Suddenly the hill avalanched—
We flailed our hands—
Fingers tangled in branches and vines—

Sand sifted over us—Sand choked
our throats—My love grew sleepy
beneath our blanket of sand…

His brother managed to crawl
from his own ruined cave.
We heard his stuttered words—

*I'm trying to dig through your roof—
Shaking too hard—His later report:
Walked miles to find a farmer,*

*one promised a search and rescue,
soon as he milked
his thirty bellowing cows.*

Crows threatened to pluck out our eyes,
bugs climbed our mountain of selves,
I heard the scratch of rat claws on our pails,

and dogs—or wolves?—howl above us.
My ribs hurt and my love grows cool
for so warm a day. Dusk fell over us.

Then I heard shouts of unfamiliar men but
my mother had warned: *don't talk with strangers,
above all not at night…*

At dawn strangers dug us out.
Next day they buried my love again.
His brother and I cried for days and days…

And now I cannot recall their names…
Might it have been Straus?

Coffin Sales Soar

Death can be good
under some circumstances
for certain trades,

if not for insurance companies
or individuals who
qualify for the containers.

Expiration Dates

The painting of the barn remains
long after barn walls cave in,
the roof dissolves in vines and mud,

until the canvas is reused
or burned or trashed.

To discuss *ephemerality* is sheer cliché
as is mention of *moonlight on snow*,
this midnight's reality.

Those who create in night's insomnia
are blessed with solitude

which envelop us all in anonymity
as life melts into nothingness like snow.

Anton, My Sweet—

He lurks among birches and pines
with pencil, notebook, stethoscope,
observes how provincial ladies hope
for impossible pleasures, and writes
this girl needs something sweet.

He'd not recognize
a leftover Halloween treat,
but notes the young lady who spies
a tiny rectangle dropped by her gate
in a foreign orange wrapper
bugs cannot penetrate.

Quickened heart rate,
he records, *adrenaline on rise.*
She stoops, scatters ants.
Bitten nails rupture the wrapper.
Teeth—pearly, uneven—tear
one crimped corner.

He notes her dismay to discover
sun-melted chocolate
sticks to the paper,
exposes beige wafers
like broken bones.
She tugs the wrapper
apart the way he separates
flesh to pry shells from wounds.

She will not waste:
Russians remember
recurring famines and wars.
Her teeth scrape the substance like mud.
Then she crumples the paper. *Sedate,*
but how she licks her fingers!

Photo of the Artist as a Double Exposure

For Krishna Mustajab

Two windows in his skull:
one looks out, one looks in.
Sun slides inside and galaxies pour forth.

Shiny panes are barred to keep out
the ant who dares
creep up his photograph.

Stairs sprout from his head—
His pate sacred, those stairs climb toward God.
Branches flower with his blood.

A ghost lurks near his shoulder—
The artist keeps his ghost behind his back
to remind him how much work to do before he dies.

But that ghost laughs!
Because he painted love in fifty colors?
Does he laugh at death? Or at me?

His eyes are solemn…Why do they swallow me?
I do not know.
I did not know.

My Twenty-Ninth Draft:

another ars poetica

I tweak it again.
Each time I pick it up, click it in:
something to change/add/delete.

My characters must be tired of
being pushed around— T'hell
with them. I'm in charge.

Except when I'm not
and my dramatis personae
take off in their own directions.

Can't chase them, rein them in,
drag them home like dulcet cows.
No paths back.

Best I can do:
describe their wild trips,
clean up in their wake.

II

Country Matters

Trying to Make Connections

Eating dusty blueberries
watching a dusty freighter rip
the rind of the bay
waves reknitting her wake, the shade
of blueberries topped
with whipped cream,

Thinking: rooted, rootless,
all in motion, though
blueberry bushes don't
sway much, but wait to be
plucked, pruned or moved.

What connection? Mine,
while I eat dusty berries,
watch the dusty freighter.

Viewed through a pane
as if in a photograph
nothing is reliable, real:
sea unstable beyond
unstable dunes,
dune grass bent, trampled, crushed,
dependent on weather to change
from straw into green.

Ephemeral fruit,
impermanent ship,
overly-metaphored sea,
the present continuous,

nothing fixed in limiting space while
extending through limitless time.

Blueberries and freighter
vanish into past tense.

We Wake Beside an Invisible River

Fog erases Georgia pines
screens our world inside a Japanese dawn,
veils deer among flowering quince.

Yet through the scrim of mists
we will see the Buddha at Kamakura,
small deer we fed at Nara,

and cormorants with rings
around their throats bringing fish
to skiffs in the Inland Sea.

When mists melt, we will see Fujiyama
surrounded by sapphire waves
and crowned with perpetual snows—

But the tardy sun burns this day clear
over our own gray-green cove—
Tide covers our marshes and sand.

Our great blue heron proclaims longevity
as he overflies cattails and huge pink
marshmallow flowers edging the cove.

The cormorant passing through dives
for minnows, swallows them down his long neck
then, perched on a piling, airs his long narrow wings.

The far river banks are fringed with bent oaks
between fields of soybeans and pastures where
ebony steers graze beside our briny Patuxent river,

One crane flies against the misty red sun
over a rice padi, pink petals, thin reeds,
on an antique scroll on our Maryland wall.

Winged Visitations, April Midnight

Two tiny figure skaters on air
pirouette around
the hanging light:

Miniature moths? Butterflies?
First of this tardy spring,
heralds of summer!

No. *Ants*, in nuptial ballet.
Harbingers of hordes
set to begin domesticity here.

Both drop on my page.
Not what most people do
but I'll free them outdoors—

Yet they already seem half-expired…
so I pinch the tiny thoraxes,
drop them into the trash.

Wings of guilt at killing
a creature forever flicker
through empty air…

Exoskeletons

Tiny claws cling to my finger.
I snatch the chance to monitor
a cicada shedding ivory armor.
Human guests don't linger.

Head first…Extra-large, wide-set hat pin eyes.
Gender? Neither of us knows which.
How soon till it flies?
Diaphanous bridal-veil wings twitch—

So I dare to say *she*, though to identify
with bugs has limits: I'd not want to spend
seventeen years underground, like a wingless fly,
a nymph left there to fend

alone, awash in horrid anal fluids and
prey to cold, moles and flood
while thorax and waist expand, expand,
shed and grow in the mud

under unseen moons and suns,
no guidelines, still unsure of which sex,
unskilled at counting seasons,
life going on above me. Mine as complex.

I watch
        one final split of her ivory shield…
                Claws detach—
                        she's off over the field—

What drives her engine
toward what she cannot conceive? Too
anthropomorphic. Still, I imagine
more than mere hunger for oak leaves…

Neither of us can predict what's to come,
but escaped from that hole, in flight
she is freed to sing and drum
all day and all night—

One hitch:
Music-making reserved for the male:
"Only males hit the right pitch."
Again, we females fall…

And she leaves the answer
to which buzz is *hers*
among multiple buzzers,
like all else, uncertain…

Strange Nightly Visitors

misshapen wolves
snatch the lambs of day
don't sleep   won't let me

they lack corporeal   substance
      still malevolent   they
infiltrate insomnia

faces malleable as   plasticine
these humanoids flash by
grins   obscene

ballooning lips   offer
      invitations   fat
fingers   beckon

I won't investigate
won't follow
hope   to wake   in time

Trying to Nab Him

So what if he cannot bring to mind
the square root of Pi,
this roach on the fly
knows his miniature brain
is better than mine,
knows I am trying again—

> In Penang, I coexisted all night
> with a cockroach six-inches high:
> he read over my elbow while
> by Coleman lamp I tried to write.
> Come dawn, he departed. So did I
> and wrote the tale of that midnight.

Tonight's inch-long Maryland drone
barely engenders a line.

On the floor, alone,
he slips into a hole
where he will abide
his own cockroach time...

When Foxes Came Calling

1. My First Fox

To this old house in the woods, he comes between red sun and night, his ruff tinged rust with leftover glow. Could he know dusk his color, his hour, as for mouse, mole and vole who scurry through tunnels which lace our lawn in subterranean webs.

I'd like to think he may think, (if he thinks so altruistically, despite some rule against anthropomorphism in literature), he does us a favor by policing our scruffy yard by the river.

He steps among tiger lilies, alert for whoever slips past underfoot, his bottlebrush tail still as a stick. He eavesdrops, suddenly leaps—pounces—nabs wind—Lands with a look which admits he has been outfoxed by a mouse, mole or vole.

2. Our Twin Foxes

Unlike Ted Hughes' imaginary fox, ours are real, not similes or stand- ins for tricky academic ideas and metaphors. Juveniles, bibs white against rusty collars as if invited for a formal tea party—

Through our glass door Pusscat studies the visitors who are aware I too am an observer. Neither Pusscat nor I twitch…Dish clean, both foxes turn, like ideas completed, stashed for further examination, expanding upon or discarding the next afternoon. I slide the door. Pusscat bounds down the four crumbling brick stairs, chases the invaders across the yard to the woods, then, satisfied, she returns.

Next day at four, the foxes reappear. Their visits continue. How to
freeze them into static metaphors! But wily, they stay alive until
this summer's end, then they disappear...

Shots resound! Hunting season open. They surely dove into dens
up our dirt lane, darted through woods to safer groves— They
don't reappear...Like our thoughts: foxy lines forgotten...

3. Why No Foxes Now?

My foxes are not metaphors but unseen critters who patrol other
woods. Rabbits have returned since last fox vanished four years
ago. Foxes should be sneaking back, gold eyes glimpsed in head-
lights, flash of tail spied across the yard—

What is the parallel for which this could be metaphor? An idea,
brilliant plot? Notes unheard but inside a composer's skull and
meant to grow into a symphony? Remember *La Boheme* where
Marcello and Rudolfo burn Act III in the empty stove...

Think of prisoners plunked on an Indonesian isle, no pencils, pens
or paper, only sticks to write on sand. In thick-walled prisons,
Solzhenitsyn wrote his lines on toilet paper, Mandelstam's fellow
inmates memorized his poems.

Even my fictional Caldecott, captive in a cell and cage,
his sole companion a mouse or rat—tries in solitude—

At least *I* have a pen, a tatter of tissue wide enough...
I'm grateful for these gifts, solitude, and paw prints
on my brain.

Between Two Thunderstorms: Floricultural Traditions

*reading Foreign Policy dispatches from the Middle East
regarding both massacres and so-called natural disasters*

A break to carry eggshells, orange rinds and carrot peels to
the bin at the edge of the woods, contemplate detritus of
our lives, and rinse my holey sneakers in the puddles.

This gray dawn, beyond the garage where no one goes,
they'd not give an anthropomorphic damn whether
anyone passes and pauses.

First of this spring…Nobody will miss them if I pick…

Lilies are blooming metaphors to buttress the cliché
that life, if not always love, is limited. Time, unstable
days and seasons, etc. They might muse on their own
blatant sexuality: pistils and stamens thrust into the
dawn as if no tomorrow. They can't know there's not.

I reach through briars—But two? Russian tradition:
an even count of flowers in a vase means someone
has died, an odd number honors the living…

I won't invite Death, already too frequent a guest,
but will add both miniature daffodils to the lone
narcissus on my sill. None will last beyond sunset,
their colors orange and yellow, streaked with blood.

Cherry, apple, pear and plum trees, their blossoms
infinite, even and odd, celebrate the living, honor
the dead who live on in these funeral wreaths in sky.

I pick, an ephemeral offering for you. Let us open, bloom while we can. By dark we too wither, drop.

A muskrat dashes from the cove ashore, prophet of reality.

A Real Big Mother Terrapin—

A carapace the size of our cast-iron frying pan,
the first turtle of this summer, today August 1 —
and in recent years all turtles scarce —
lumbers from the swamp beyond the small garage
up the stones and through the poison ivy.

Not stretching her long neck to glance back
she heads non-stop across the lawn toward
the far woods to lay her eggs…

She'll dig a hole in the lawn, or farther swamp,
maybe two or three holes to confuse us, then
pump out eggs like ping-pong balls—But where?

No foxes this year, and no raccoon or possum
as yet to show, so none might dig the eggs.

I'll nurture these, then in a couple of months,
while waving off bald eagles, gulls, I will
escort the hatchlings to the shore—

I glance up to watch two vultures overhead.

When I look down again: no sign of her…

Natural Questions

How do our oaks know
when to drop acorns in autumn,
and deer know they must vacuum
up every acorn before December?

And the squirrels who have eaten
or hidden in their secret larders
every apple on our tree—
Do they too foresee a long winter?

Not always the fittest survive.
The squirrel who daily limps to the door
is a moth-eaten cross-eyed runt
but he knows I'm a soft touch and here:

as the real estate agent reiterates,
Location, location, that is what counts.

Fifty Beans

I ignore the *Almanac*,
don't wait until the next
dark of the moon but,
summer drought is already on us,
cruel as ache and age,

between sunset and the rise
of a bean-shaped moon
I plant fifty bush-bean seeds:
half-inch, whitish, oblong,
like my pain-relieving pills.

Will these seeds hatch
to hardy seedlings, stretch
anxious tendrils, bush out full?
Will the promised crop
grow purple-green and tall?

Or will squirrels dig them up,
the seeds rot unseen,
weeds smother the whole patch,
beans turn out duds
like my pills?

Cake-Eaters

All I have to scatter along
the snowy balcony rail is what
I can scratch from this brick—
once a sponge cake but
long forgotten in
the over-stocked fridge.

Could scrape with a grater—

None at hand, so by hand
I crunch chunks for a feast
fit for a peacock,
pterodactyl, firebird, or
angel with a sweet tooth…

Only sparrows land. Black-
throated, striped, fox
sparrows, song, plain.
Underbirds of the phylum,
street-sweepers, poor kids
raiding a toys-for-tots bin
for last Halloween's chocolates,
riffling for coins in a dead mother's desk.

Thoughtless, not yet headless, Antoinette
announced the poor could eat cake.

So till blue jays, cardinals and catbirds,
push each other from the balcony rail,
let sparrows scavenge, and feast.

Arboreal

One leaf in the tree too far to identify
twirls and twists in its own wind,
may wither, brown, fall with the rest
or keep its own schedule.

No need for comparison,
labels "metaphor" or "simile."
This leaf *is*, I *am*, will merely attempt
to keep watch, keep on twirling, twisting—

Farmer's Almanac Forecasts

a blizzard will cover the daffodils
which struggle months to work their way
through soil like lava from Earth's core,

daffodils like lives born underneath the soil—
beetles, grubs and moles, who make it
through the muck.

Their endo- and exo-skeletons
pile high as if to hide
their lives, and ours.

Gardeners in Flight

The earth we dug, seeded, tended, pruned,
before harvest were forced to abandon—

Will those who take over our land
pour dregs of their tea over our seeds,
pray over our seedlings, bless whatever grows,
pull weeds, preserve the seeds for next year?

We are all refugees, Eve but the first.

Banished, did she create a plot,
scratch furrows, sow patches of desert
to be fertilized by blood
from that first fratricide?

Can we?

You Missed Two Young Bald Eagles Practicing Flight at Dawn over our Cove

You will miss our eagles, herons, gulls,
our aviary- worth of inland birds, including sparrows
God's too busy to look after so gives me the job.

You will miss complaining about
their scattered crumbs, seeds, and droppings
repainting our balcony with a Jackson Pollack.

You'll miss damning the squirrels who
clean up whatever birds miss; you'll miss
complaining about my piled manuscripts,

my cluttered 1998 Subaru, my swiping for
the wash your clothes worn day and night,
and your orange peels to mulch

my garden which fed us ten years
though now you won't let me plant
now you want more scruffy grass to mow.

You will miss eternally complaining
about apricots you can't see because
they are right before your eyes,

and all else you see or don't, but
like everything you choose
to keep you awake all night, bug you.

You will, in short, miss living…So
will I, along with all else I cannot
live without, including you…

III

Foreign Affairs

"Like a flame from the hearth, Love…"

Hilary Tham

Those flames have warmed me,
singed me, burned me, left me
charred by the side of the road.

But, phoenix or salamander, I
shake free of cinders.

Winds blow off the ash
leave me grayed.

When winds turn cold
I discover another hearth,
campfire in the desert—

a candle flame will suffice
and I am on fire again.

Infolding

I might take you inside me
for a while
although aware

of your departure at dawn
my flooded emptiness
ephemerality

Best you slip me through a slit
in your own belly
thrust me high beneath your ribs

Implanted talisman
I'll curl in your dim cage
a creature hibernating

or fetus growing big against
your disconcerted maleness
I'll beat my head against your walls

But keep me in till my flesh
melts into your own
and my bones fuse with yours

Egg-Collecting

Eluding watchdogs, spies,
we steal like foxes, gray and red,
inside the henhouse—

Locked like barracks until dawn.
Hens scatter, cluck.
White, mottled, brown—

They ignore the theories
of relations incompatible between
birds of different feathers.

And they're accommodating:
They rise from nests
like prisoners' beds of straw.

We reach beneath angora chests
to snatch warm eggs
(white, mottled, brown).

They settle back, feathered robots
to fill tomorrow's norm.
We won't be here tomorrow.

We cradle speckled treasures now.
A brooding hen, my breasts
are nestling eggs, clutch

the source of life, ellipsoidal, delicate.
Each egg forms one huge cell.
Invisible in me, one tiny egg…

This waits, unfertilized...
Beneath a microscope, would its yolk
be as bright? The rind, more vulnerable...

We dust off feathers, straw, clean,
pierce both ends of shells,
then with one vacuum gulp—

We suck them alive inside our mouths—
Orange yolks, still whole,
slide down our throats.

Now you as well contain an egg—
Sturgeon, woman, shad—O rooster!
You smother me in feathers...

At cockcrow you'll fly home,
muted far beyond barbed wire,
while I brood growing cells...

- - -

Do You See Colors Coming?
Wrote a Would-be Lover

In a foreign land, I had to burn
his letters quickly before anyone—
Thirty years later I still see
blue ink his wide-nibbed fountain pen
incised across the charred page.

Today the ophthalmologist squeezes
drops through my unwilling lids—
They sting like fire!
He flashes a spectrum of lights
in my cobwebbed eyes.
White incandescent neon, glowing gold…

Pain fades like old loves
but leaves rainbows and after-prints
indigo, emerald, magenta,
bright as in sun-struck cathedrals—
Such colors! What if unwittingly I'm coming?

The doctor sees only the gold.
Hairy-fingered, boulder-bald, he knows
from medical texts the Fourth of July in my eyes:

Fireworks more dazzling than any the Chinese
invented could mean my retina's come unstuck,
portend his hand on a laser gun—
But, optimistic about my condition,
he instructs: "Wear dark glasses,
return in three months."

As for my long-ago correspondent,
who later became more
than a gleam in the eye,
I never saw colors with him.

Setting History Straight

Goliath had more going for him:
height, weight, vocal power, bronze duds,
while David sought inspiration in the arts
and physics, gained a better press.

What's not recorded, or got lost
in all those translations:
the hitman of the Philistines
was merely stunned by David's stone
and his neck proved too thick to hack.

A wild ass passing by licked
the bloody face and neck till he awoke,
his migraine fierce as Yahweh's wrath.

In a mountain cave,
pain left him drumming fat
fingers on the shaft of his spear.

He waited, calm as a toad
with growing appetite
until that upstart
strumming his flimsy lyre
strolled past the dark cloaca of cave.

The end was swift as
a turtle snapping a gadfly.
Goliath gulped the twerp,
then sat back, satisfied.

The moral of the tale:
In the power game, you try and try.
If at first you don't succeed,
tinker with history. Might rewrites.

Tradecraft: Finding a Safe House for a Begonia

"Home is a dangerous place," PK said

Your father beat you as a child.
Your aging mother shuns you now.
Moribund brothers welcome you home
as long as they need a chauffeur.

Wives and beloveds come, disappear,
return like starlings in mid-migration—
more like vultures who hover overhead,
descend when they need a feast.

Yet you built a safe house in your heart
for the homeless on all our doorsteps,
you recite incantations, new alphabets,
weave words into blankets, or shrouds.

Christmas Eve you bring to this safe house
one cyclamen, covert messages traced
on forest green heart-shaped leaves,
codes in petals magenta as love.

Our Housemate from India Asks

When should I bring the potted plants inside?
Jayita Sarkar

When our Hunter's Moon is full
but gives no heat

When back home your moon's full too
and they celebrate
Laxmi puja, goddess of wealth

Here, when time here to wear
unfamiliar coats

When stink bugs steal indoors
to share our warmth

With apologies we flick them out
not on our conscience if
they die from cold

When October spiders spin
webs to snare leftover flies
Arachnids on the payroll

When, as Pushkin wrote,
"November stands on the threshold"

When time to want lovers in our beds

Does this answer your question?

"Psychiatrists Inspect Your Purse"
You Warn as You Scribble a Name on My Handkerchief

I avoid shrinks but just in case, better dump
    expired calendars, uncashed checks, unpaid bills,
    receipts for shoes which no longer fit, toothless combs,
    broken pencils, spent pens, loose keys for forgotten doors,
    unidentifiable pills, coins from unmapped lands,
    illegible addresses whose owners
    I cannot remember or would rather forget…

    Someone's cufflink I promised to fix decades ago!

    Ah, sugar lumps swiped from forgotten cafes
    (never know when we'll need something sweet),

Quick, everything into the trash—

Wait! What unwritten stories lurk here?

I shake grit and crumbs from my purse,
put the rest back with new pencils, pens,
paper, Chanel #5…One fixed cufflink:
someday I will find its mate, and mine.

Only the grayed handkerchief with your shrink's
ink-smudged number goes in the wash, with bleach.

Old Housemates

He stays locked in the attic closet
though he left the house years ago,
bolted the door.

The lady down the street whose big droopy breasts, he told me intrigued him, finally wed him.

They did not invite me
to that ceremony
or to his funeral.

Thus I'm protected
from too many ghosts
as long as he stays
locked away.

Real Estate Stationary

Willy-nilly we adapt to new
estates wherever and however.
Reality waits and drools.

We attempt to outsmart history,
retrieve our hovels/palaces/estates,
but know that change is real.

If my babushka's estate
amid those distant groves
stood real today, unburned despite

years of revolutions, famines, wars,
exile, unexpected travels, still more wars,
that real estate might be mine.

But in many lands
every year brings change
of regime, venue, self.

So, invisible or hard to miss,
we carry history
on our unguarded backs

like turtles through the marsh
guided by unseen compasses
year after year, same turf to dig

A DOG in my SPAM!

A virtual dog at my real door
scratching and whining until he's a bore—

Wants to be fed, then taken to run
in the stratosphere until he is done

then catch a can of Spam (I found a few
left over from World War Two)

since without gravity virtual Kibbles
float and freeze aloft to ice-bubbles.

The galaxy a borderless alley
neither beginning nor a finale

so the online canine gets infinite exercise
chasing his airy dinner to paradise—

Now all he's left behind are his bark
and my real need to clean up the park.

"Legs and Toes in Ancestor of Living Snakes"

New York Times, May 19, 2015

Another Darned Eve Poem of Which
There Are Many in Which the Poet
Compares Herself with the Very First Lady

Sent from the Garden, did Eve not complain?
No need there to ask Adam, "Please rake the leaves,
pull those weeds." God made each plant grow
and shed for a purpose, part of His plan, in there.

Out here, God may let "weeds" grow,
spent leaves fall, mulch where they land,
to keep us bobbing, bowing, burning—

In the Garden, Eve needn't fear snakes
or mice, snakes had no need to catch.
Critters there never ran out of food
nor did Adam and Eve.

Beyond the bountiful Garden,
she bore one troublesome son.

As did I. At least, in my garden,
mine will rake leaves and pull weeds.
And he plays with snakes
with or without their limbs.

Those Lights

"It's the lights across the bay
I'll miss the most—" sighs
fictional Aunt Eleanora
in my half-written book.

She sips dark rum
from her chipped cup,
gold-rimmed Limoges,
and closes dimming eyes.

With my own dimming eyes
I treasure those few lights
in the trailer park
across our shallow cove.

Who keeps lights on at 2 a.m.
when they should sleep?
Do they, too, drink to fall asleep
or stay awake to party?

I drink real rum in milk
the way that my invented
great aunt drank, to sleep…

Skullduggery

My ailing publisher asked me not
for one more manuscript.
"Just your collection of skulls."

Fox skull, sheep skull, mouse,
water buffalo with horns like scimitars,
my prized Malaysian boar?

The human cranium I found
spilled from a churchyard, gravestones worn
beyond decoding, down to a cold
New Brunswick beach beneath
eroding bluffs—
how could I abandon this trophy?

Did he plan, like St. Jerome,
to meditate upon those fleshless heads?

Finger eye sockets to envision
a boneless bookless heaven where
writers, critics, editors,
blue-penciled out eternity in peace?

Did he inquire when Death—

But that spineless guest
gave him no time to mail
my borrowed skulls.

Those who incinerated him
to spare a skeletal infinity,
and cleared up after him,
did they throw out
his treasures with his trash?

I need them now.

Today the Roofer—

Repaired my stapler: tiny wires caught in the slot meant I could not cinch the bills for the new roof, or much else in my disjointed life.

All it took him was a fork to open the stapler so not just the cap but all three parts spread like legs. Now I could pry three jammed staples free. They scattered, then the whole pack.

Also the cherry tree, which grew from a pit spat over the balcony into our patch of dirt, burst into bloom and scattered myriad petals.

Without being asked the roofer cleared petals and dead leaves.

Granted I poured sugar into his tea (in my silver-handled glass instead of a Styrofoam cup) and served in a blue-and-white bowl home-made soup (chicken, onions, carrots, potatoes, beets, though garlic and chili powder for his Latin tastes meant I no longer could call it borsht); plus grilled cheese, mangoes, bananas, cookies, cake.

Anything better than Big Macs and fries, he brings to other jobs.

He is thirty-two, I'm not, but when we'd added all his receipts

for bundled shingles, tarpaper rolls, pounds of nails and screws, paint for eaves, brushes, flashing, gutters, downspouts, then six trips to the dump in his battered, red pickup, his hours of work, my English slowed to make sure he had understood, and I had written checks while he packed hammer, drills, wrenches, saws, and extra-strong plastic bags, he drank his sweet black tea, kissed my hand, took both my hands in his, kissed me on both cheeks.

Trampled weeds may not survive. Lost staples, rusty screws, plastic-capped nails, tarpaper scraps, shards of rotted shingles, will remain for years in that patch of dirt below my balcony. His kiss will last as long as the roof, guaranteed for 25 years.

Dissolution Rates: The Mouse in the Toilet

Escaped from Yale's Alzheimer Lab
up north in New Haven?
Injected with meds to create
"a cascade of molecular
and cellular interactions"?

Yet with the proper drugs, he might
swim and climb from the water,
up the slippery sides, shake dry
his fur, run free if drunkenly—

Too late: thoroughly dead.
Home-grown in this house.
God's said to care for sparrows.
What about mice? Was this *my* job?

I flush once, when the tank refills,
flush again to make sure.

His bones will remain
in cesspool or drain until
they dissolve…But when?

I Google science sites:
In *human* bones,
rate of dissolution varies.

Too many younger friends popping off,
interments, cremations, dissolutions,
best *I* die far from research labs,
in a warm and welcoming ocean.

May my bones buck up
the calcium in fishes' spines,
no funny drugs in my brain
to muck up the water.

Galaxy: Another Archetypal Love Poem

Likewise existing for infinity

and since nothing marks the spark
or will it end in sparks

or deadly banalities
of dishwater dumped in a ditch,

ours was, is, will be.

Pushing Through the Night

For William Rivera

We push through darkened halls
unsure if we will find a moonlit room
or crash into the table's edge
and scrape our elbows raw again.

We try to staunch this blood,
replenish bandages and salves,
keep on weaving, stumbling,
falling through the night—

Relentless Mind:

Burning, burning—

the yellow anti-bug bulb
not bright enough to read by,
not clear enough to clarify,
nor warm,

yet burning, burning—

When I find the switch to turn it off
the outer mechanism falls apart,
the inner—

I can't reach.

After Departures

Guests gone, I sit with three cats
on a couch still warm from a man

I would like to have loved
and a woman who drank too much.

Monsoons this midnight: he will not
reappear. A tree broke over the road.

The kitten is hitting a Christmas tree
ball although it's already May.

Sometimes I have trouble putting away
souvenirs from a previous season.

Cat Tracks

You're off. Tomcatting. I'm left,
fish bones in my guts.
Did I rub your unruly fur the wrong way?
Do old scars disfigure my ears?

Then I too will track alleys.
Even now, other toms sniff my scent:
since you departed, I've had
six lovers in recurrent cycles—

All elegant passionate toms.
Might I, a striped alley queen,
litter six kittens all at one birth
each by a different sire?

Tonight while I waited for
the red light to change to green
a white-haired gentleman tom
complimented me on my coat.

I showed him my claws,
scurried over the curb.
But I miss *our* cacophonous nights
so much I could stoop to him,

for though fish makes me sick
and I get dizzy in trees,
I've developed a taste for oysters
and penthouse roofs.

Yet if I tumbled off,
would I find my eight other lives?
For I understand now
you won't be there to catch me.

Crossing the Field

Despite a toothache, I'm walking over the fields.
Tuesday at 8:00 my younger son may be jailed.

Scaring quail, I head toward the briars,
maroon shoots hairy with thorns, to stake
my claim to poor-man's wineberries.

Like mothers from Persia to El Salvador, I complain
of pain, mourn my suddenly dangerous son,
stumble on clods upheaved like miniature
horsts and grabens on war-torn battlefields…

He used to carry the pail and recite my poems
as we crossed these fields to pick berries for jam…

Now 16, he sassed a cop and faces a lock up.
In another land, he'd be jailed or shot.

Alfalfa, ploughed under, will nourish new crops.

Neither this hurt in my mouth nor pain in my heart
will nourish anything.

An Aerial Ballet

Naughty in the wind, my safety net a web,
with spider strands I'm stringed to you—

Heights terrify, my tightrope wants
to strangle me—
The spider counts my stumbles.

But you dare me pirouette on parapets,
twirl on marble balustrades,
cross chasms without tightropes, leap—

You worry I'll break loose and disappear—

I am scared you might let go the reel…

Determinations

Snow continues to pile up
while we slog toward
closed airports.

My angora escapes again
to her tawdry tom,
another bellyful of kittens.

Sightless, mindless, the crone
tied in the Home's restraining chair
twists till she's free on the floor.

Somehow, we insist
on getting where we're going.

Discussing Olympus at Camelot Hall Nursing Home
[the residents speak, if they can]

What anachronistic Grecian gods
can help us now? What myths explain
Promethean livers, wounded heels,
spent bones, one unpaired eye?

Those gods an under-thirty bunch
except Poseidon, that old salt,
like Orpheus they are too
preoccupied to be debriefed.

Athena has abandoned us.
Aphrodite mouths a tawdry joke.
Zeus turns to new pursuits.

Persephone still breezes past,
won't share one pomegranate seed.
Demeter's on the shelf.

Only bovine Io understands
indignity of change, incontinence,
bellowed helplessness,
this pastured lack of grace.

Icarus, you were in luck.
We'd trade these wheelchairs
for your wings, despite the cost.
We cherish dreams of immortality—

Mere hallucinations.
We've had experience with risk
and shattered plans.

We'd like the business done.

August at the County Landfill

Dismembered toys, rotted planks, ripped bags,
weigh down my '97 Subaru which sags amid the flat-beds,
eighteen-wheelers, raging bulldozers. We chuck
another load the monster grinder chafes to crush.

Odors spill from mounds of garbage, rags,
discarded junk. A sweaty tractor driver ties
a blue bandana bandit-style against the dust—
as if cloth blocked out scents and clangs and flies.

Gulls patrol the parapets, dive to nab their lunch.
Forty gargoyles drop like plastic sacks, morph into
Black Vultures—These balance, hump, flaunt
wings five feet across, prance on bins, sniff—

Haunting fragrances persist! Let future archaeologists
smell out the fossil prints of claws and feathers shed
by sooty choirs of fallen angels sent to check artifacts
of Envy, Gluttony and Greed stay in the dump—

Credo

> *"aku melasa jemu kepada segi empat"*
> *"I'm sick of the square"*
>
> Krishna Mustajab

Yes, let's shatter the square
slice rectangles to shards
slash rhomboids
knead trapezoids
till corners like horns
rise through our fists
explode to shredded space

spare nothing geometrical
toss the fragments on a grid
at intervals of sound
from suffering strings inside
interstices squeezed till they weep

splash this collage with blood
red from our hearts
blue from my veins
black from your eyes
white from a marbled moon

decorate with slips of skin
peeled in the search
for greater nakedness

until we reach the onion's core
and exist no more

only art remains

Author's Note

Elisavietta Ritchie's prose, poetry, photographs, translations are widely published, translated, and anthologized in the United States and abroad. Credits include *The New York Times, The Washington Post, Poetry, American Scholar, The Christian Science Monitor, JAMA: Journal of the American Medical Association, Canadian Woman Studies, Confrontation, Potomac Review*, and numerous other publications.

Tightening the Circle Over Eel Country won the Great Lakes Colleges Association's "New Writer's Award, 1975–1976." Individual poems and stories won awards from the Poetry Society of America, National Endowment for the Arts, The Ledge, Bright Hill Press, and others. Several were nominated for the Pushcart Prize.

Ritchie writes, translates, edits, gives readings, workshops, serves as poet-in-the-schools, and helps writers of various ages. She was long active with the Washington Writers' Publishing House, where, after winning annual awards for a book of poetry and later of fiction, she served first as president of the poetry then the fiction division. She also created The Wineberry Press to publish others' manuscripts too unconventional for regular presses.

She traveled to several continents independently and as a Visiting Overseas Speaker for the United States Information Service. Her most recent collection from Poets' Choice Publishers is *Reflections: Poems on Paintings, A Poet's Gallery*; readings of these poems can be accompanied with the paintings (most of which are at The National Gallery) which inspired them on PowerPoint.

Ritchie has been nurturing poets, painters, musicians and wildlife, and writing on the shores of the Patuxent River, Maryland, the Potomac, Washington DC, and rivers and seacoasts of Cyprus, Malaysia, the Balkans, Australia, Canada and briefly, the USSR and the African continent.